Collins

easy learning

a b c
workbook

Ages 3–5

apple

boat

cat

Carol Medcalf

How to use this book

- Find a quiet, comfortable place to work, away from distractions.

- This book has been written in a logical order, so start at the first page and work your way through.

- Working through this book, your child will start to realise that words are made up of small separate sounds. These individual sounds are called phonemes; bus, for example, is made up of three phonemes: b-u-s. Encourage your child to say the individual letter sounds to make words.

- Help with reading the instructions where necessary and ensure that your child understands what to do.

- When questions have two parts, it is often best to gain the first answer and record it before moving on to the next part of the question.

- If an activity is too difficult for your child then do more of our suggested practical activities (see Parent's tip) and return to the page when you know that they're likely to achieve it.

- Some children find it easier if all the other activities on the page are covered with a blank piece of paper, so only the activity they are working on is visible.

- Always end each activity before your child gets tired so that they will be eager to return next time.

- Help and encourage your child to check their own answers as they complete each activity.

- Let your child return to their favourite pages once they have been completed. Talk about the activities they enjoyed and what they have learnt.

Special features of this book:

- **Parent's tip:** situated at the bottom of every left-hand page, this suggests further activities and encourages discussion about what your child has learnt.

- **Progress panel:** situated at the bottom of every right-hand page, the number of animals and stars shows your child how far they have progressed through the book. Once they have completed each double page, ask them to colour in the white star.

- **Certificate:** the certificate on the inside back cover should be used to reward your child for their effort and achievement. Remember to give them plenty of praise and encouragement, regardless of how they do.

Published by Collins
An imprint of HarperCollins*Publishers* Ltd
The News Building
1 London Bridge Street
London
SE1 9GF

Browse the complete Collins catalogue at www.collins.co.uk

© HarperCollins*Publishers* Ltd 2013
This edition © HarperCollins*Publishers* Ltd 2015

10 9 8 7 6 5 4 3 2 1

ISBN 978-0-00-815151-5

Written by Carol Medcalf
Page layout by Linda Miles, Lodestone Publishing and Contentra Technologies Ltd
Illustrated by Jenny Tulip
Cover design by Sarah Duxbury and Paul Oates
Cover illustration by John Haslam
Project managed by Chantal Peacock and Sonia Dawkins

MIX
Paper from responsible sources
FSC™ C007454

Contents

The alphabet sounds

● Say the sounds for each letter. Colour a box when you get the sound right. Can you do this on 3 different days and colour 3 boxes for each letter?

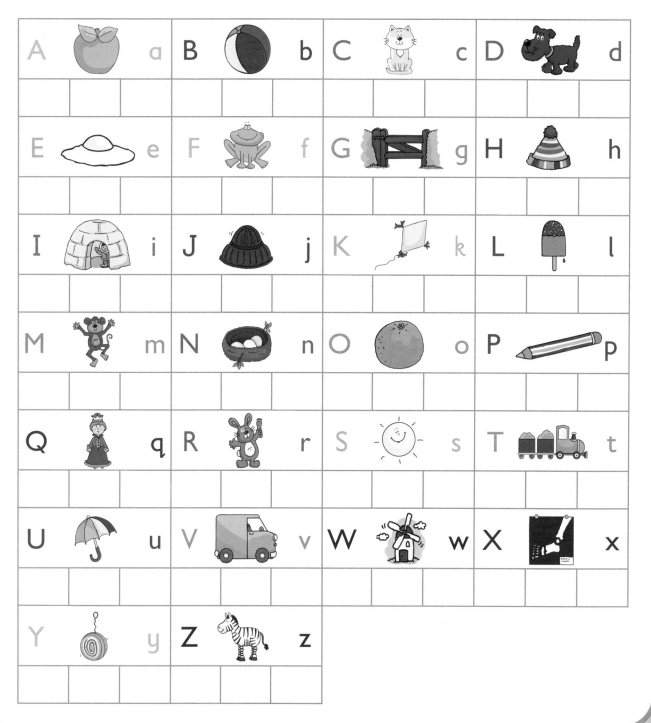

Letter sounds a–i

- Draw lines to match these letters to the picture that starts with the same sound.

a

b

c

d

e

f

g

h

i

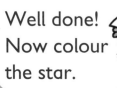

Letter sounds j–r

● Match these letters to the picture that starts with the same sound.

j

k

l

m

n

o

p

q

r

Letter sounds s–z

● Match these letters to the pictures.

s
t
u
v
w
x
y
z

Well done!
Now colour
the next star.

Letter shapes

● Which letter fits best in the shape? Write the letter in the shape.

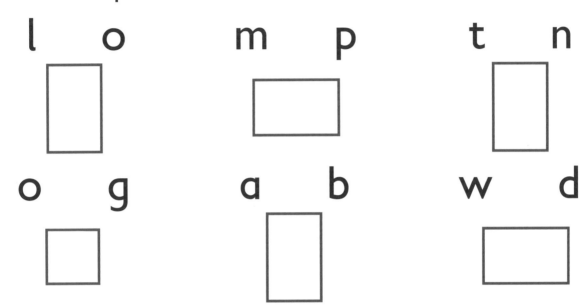

l   o   m   p   t   n

o   g   a   b   w   d

● Some letters are hiding in this picture, can you find them? Draw a circle round the letters.

To ensure your child can recognise the shapes of letters, make letters out of playdough or make biscuit letters. These can be turned into simple words, using the phonetic sounds. Repeat the sounds.

- There is an odd letter in each row, can you cross it out using ✗?

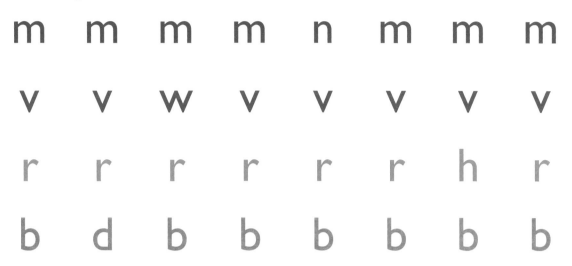

m m m m n m m m

v v w v v v v v

r r r r r r h r

b d b b b b b b

- Draw a line to match the letters that are the same in each box.

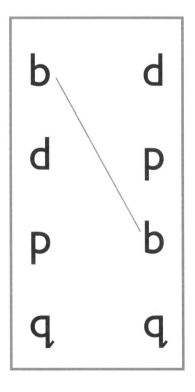

b	d
d	p
p	b
q	q

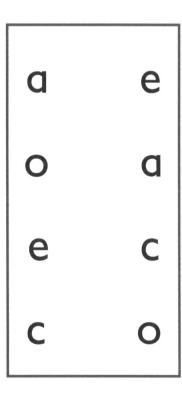

a	e
o	a
e	c
c	o

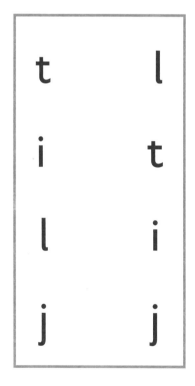

t	l
i	t
l	i
j	j

Well done! Now colour the next star.

First letter sounds

● Circle the pictures that start with the letter sound shown at the beginning of each row.

Pages 10, 11 and 20 concentrate on the letters used most often. These are often taught first in schools as they appear more than the remaining letters.

Colour the pictures that begin with these letters.

e

h

r

m

d

g

11

Three-letter words

These are called CVC words – consonant, vowel, consonant.

● Write **a** to complete these words.

 h _a_ t

 c __ t

 r __ t

 v __ n

 b __ t

 b __ g

● These words have **e** missing. Can you fill it in each word?

 b _e_ d

 t __ n

 n __ t

 p __ g

 p __ n

 l __ g

Saying each letter phonetically is the first step from learning individual letters to putting a few together to read first words. Try sounding the words out when speaking like 'Where is your l-e-g?'. 'Can you pass me the p-e-n?' Always remember to use clear phonetic sounds.

- Write **i** to finish these words.

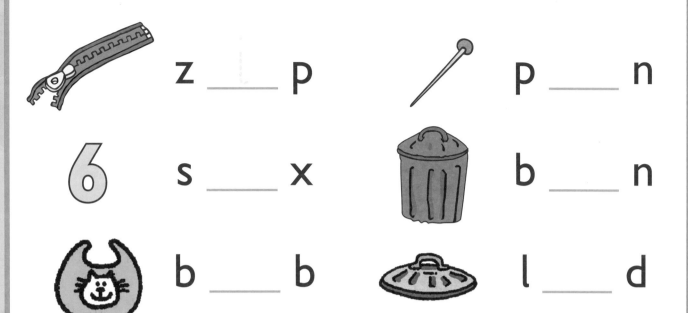

z __ p   p __ n

6   s __ x   b __ n

b __ b   l __ d

- These words are missing an **o**. Can you fill it in each word?

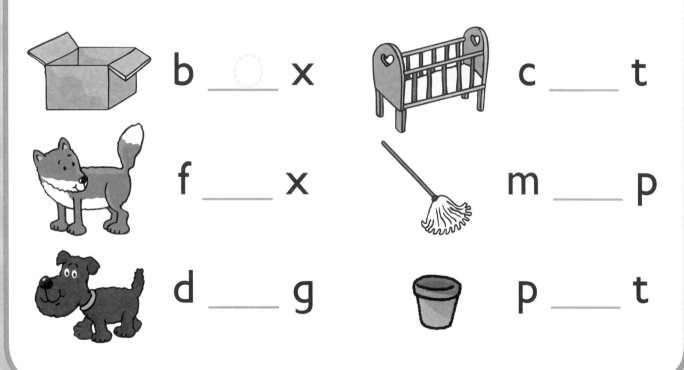

b __ x   c __ t

f __ x   m __ p

d __ g   p __ t

More three-letter words

- Write **u** to finish the words.

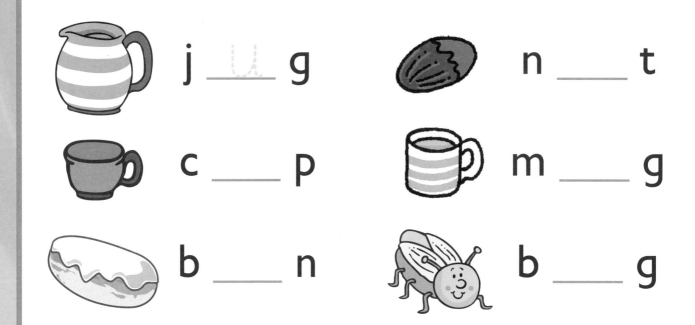

j __u__ g   n ___ t

c ___ p   m ___ g

b ___ n   b ___ g

- Which of the letters below do you need to use to finish the words? Sound the words out, can you hear the middle sound?

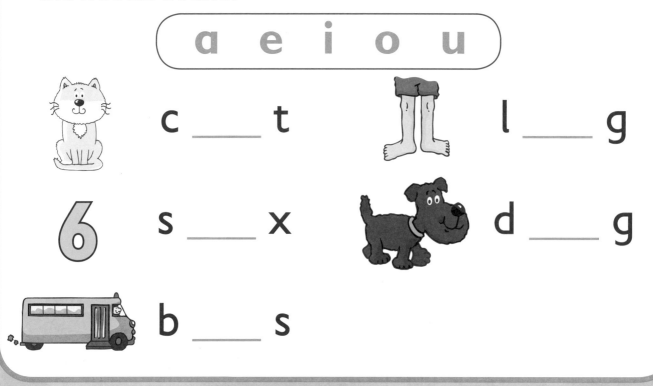

a e i o u

c ___ t   l ___ g

s ___ x   d ___ g

b ___ s

- Can you sound these letters out and hear a word? If you can, match the word to the picture.

c a t

l e g

b i n

j a m

s u n

- Now try these words.

w e b

t a p

z i p

m o p

j u g

Capital letters

● Can you match these children to their lost bags? Look at the letters on the children's t-shirts and match them to the names under the bags.

Sally   Archie   Ben   Charlie   Tegan

● Can you help these pets find their food? Look at the letters on the pets' name tags and match them to the names on the bowls.

Marley   Woody   Irene   Katie   George

It is important to learn that names always begin with a capital letter, the rest of the word is then written in lower case.

Letter match

- Can you match the capital letter to the correct lowercase letter in each box? (Look at page 4 to help you.)

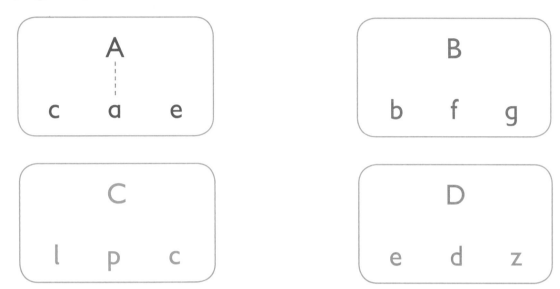

A

c   a   e

B

b   f   g

C

l   p   c

D

e   d   z

- Now try and match these lowercase letters to the correct capital letter.

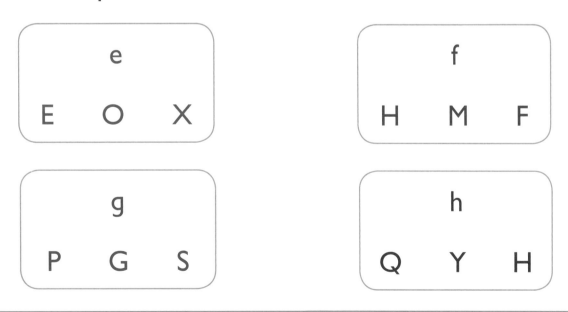

e

E   O   X

f

H   M   F

g

P   G   S

h

Q   Y   H

Well done! Now colour the next star.

Upper and lowercase letters

● Can you match the upper and lowercase letters? Look at the pictures to help you.

Write the letters of your child's name on card, like 'D a r c y'. Cut them out individually and see if they can put them back together like a jigsaw puzzle. If they like the activity, make some more using simple phonetic words. Give only one puzzle at a time so they do not get confused.

Can you match the upper and lowercase letters?
Look at the pictures to help you.

Well done!
Now colour
the next star.

First letter sounds practice

- Look at the pictures and write the first letter of each word.

_____ _____ _____ _____

_____ _____ _____

- Can you colour the fish below that have the letters found in the task above?

When a word ends in 'k', you always use 'c' before the 'k' after a vowel otherwise the word just ends in 'k', like 'fork'. All the words on page 21 show the vowel followed by 'ck'. Your child may not be ready to understand this concept yet, but it is worth knowing the rule to teach them when they are ready.

ck and ee

● Look at the pictures and write **ck** to finish the words. Can you say the **ck** sound?

so___   du___   clo___   chi___

bri___   tru___   sa___

● Look at the picture below and fill in the missing **ee** in the words. You can then read the words.

d___r

tr___

b___

sh___p   f___t   s___d

ai and oa

● Write **ai** in these words. Say the word slowly. Can you hear the sound?

 p_ _ _nt

 tr_ _ _n

 sn_ _ _l

 t_ _ _l

 ch_ _ _n

 dr_ _ _n

● Now write and say the **oa** sound.

 f_ _ _l

 g_ _ _l

 b_ _ _t

 g_ _ _t

 c_ _ _t

 r_ _ _d

Missing letters

● Can you fill in the missing letters to complete the alphabet?

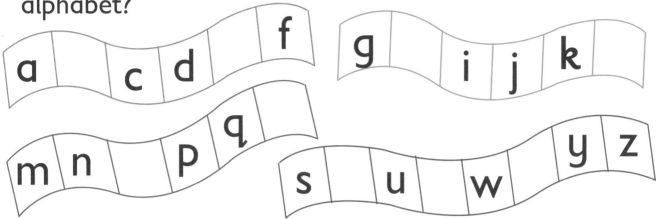

a   c   d   f   g   i   j   k

m   n   p   q   s   u   w   y   z

● What is the first letter these words begin with?
Write the letter in the box.

Well done!
Now colour
the next star.

Answers

Page 4

Child to colour a box under each letter every day that they get the sound right.

Page 5

Page 6

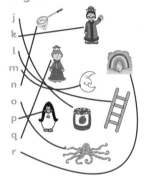

Page 7

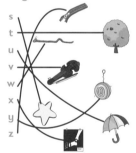

Page 8

l m t

o b w

Page 9

m m m m m ✗ m m m
v v v ✗ v v v v v
r r r r r r ✗ r
b ✗ b b b b b b

Page 10

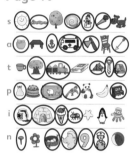

s
a
t
p
i
n

Page 11

e
h
r
m
d
g

Page 12

hat, cat, rat, van, bat, bag

bed, ten, net, peg, pen, leg

Page 13

zip, pin, six, bin, bib, lid

box, cot, fox, mop, dog, pot

Page 14

jug, nut, cup, mug, bun, bug

cat, leg, six, dog, bus

Page 15

cat
leg
bin
jam
sun

web
tap
zip
mop
jug

Page 16

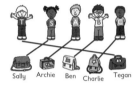

Sally Archie Ben Charlie Tegan

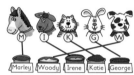

Marley Woody Irene Katie George

Page 17

| A | | B |
| c a e | | b f g |

| C | | D |
| l p c | | e d z |

| | | |
| E O X | | H M F |

| | | |
| P G S | | Q Y H |

Page 18

Page 19

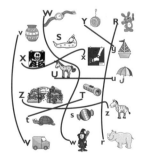

Page 20

g o u

f b

Page 21

sock duck clock chick

brick truck sack

deer   tree
bee

sheep feet seed

Page 22

paint   train
snail   tail
chain   drain

foal   goal
boat   goat
coat   road

Page 23

a b c d e f g h i j k l
m n o p q r   s t u v w x y z

w e l l   d o n e

y o u   h a v e

f i n i s h e d